WHAT'S

YOUR

PLUS

HOW TO STAND OUT WHEN YOU GRADUATE

VIHAN KHANNA

To request permissions, contact the publisher at
WhatsYourPlusBook@gmail.com.

Paperback: 978-1-7354572-0-8
Ebook: 978-1-7354572-1-5

Library of Congress Number: 2020918960

Khanna Publishing
5 Westgate Road
Livingston, NJ 07039

Table of Contents

This book is dedicated to my parents for always supporting me in any initiative I take no matter how far off the beaten path I venture.

To my sister for always being one of my greatest mentors.

And to all the friends and family who are always there to uplift and support me in my greatest moments of struggle and self-doubt.

In a world that takes pride in
being a novel,
dare to be the plot twist.

— Niti Majethia

Introduction

Imagine the following scenario. You're graduating college in a few months, and you've found a job listing for a great role—but you're likely one of thousands of applicants who meet the listed qualifications. Even within the same program at your own university, there are dozens, if not hundreds of equally qualified candidates. If you all applied for the same job, why should you expect to be picked over everyone else?

You need to stand out. And not just with good grades and a few extra-curricular activities on your resume.

Decades ago, it was possible to get a decent job just by obtaining a high school diploma while college graduates snagged the higher paying jobs. Today, almost everyone attends college or trade school after high school, so you will be competing with a large and highly educated group of applicants. Today, the job search challenges everyone.

According to the National Science Foundation, in 2018, 36.4% of Americans aged 25-44 had earned a four-year undergraduate degree. According to the National Center for Education Statistics, that's up from less than 20% in 1980. EducationData.org reports that about two million students earned a bachelor's degree in 2019, and another two million earned other post-secondary degrees. According to Glassdoor, about 250 people will apply for a job, 4-6 of them will get called back for interviews, and only one of them will get a job offer.

A higher education degree alone is no longer the sole key to the castle.

What can set you apart from all those others waving their degrees? You need something in addition to that degree, something that adds value.

You need a *plus*.

You may recognize the name Mark Cuban, the billionaire investor from the hit television show *Shark Tank*, and famously the owner of the Dallas Mavericks basketball team. However, Cuban's hustle to stand out started long before his career landed him on *Shark Tank*. As an undergraduate at Indiana University Bloomington, Cuban opened his own college bar. However, the bar was shut down due to some of its clientele being underage. Had Cuban's bar only served clients of a drinking age, it may have continued to grow and expand into a profitable business. One of his college professors even noted that they had never seen any student actually start their own business at that scale before Cuban.

After graduating in 1981, Cuban had nothing to his name except $60 cash, a pile of debt from student loans, and a floor to sleep on in a three bedroom apartment in Dallas which he shared with five other guys. Though Cuban didn't have much, he had his entrepreneurial spirit and a diverse array of experiences from his time in college. He didn't just study business in college so he could work for a business. Cuban always played by his own rules, and as a result, was destined to run his own business.

Cuban worked a number of jobs after college, all of which he got fired from or quit before starting his first enterprise, a software company called MicroSolutions. Eventually, Cuban sold Micro Solutions for six million dollars to a subsidiary of H&R Block, CompuServe. Five years later, Cuban, along with a friend, wanted to listen to Indiana Hoosier games from where they lived in Dallas, so they created broadcast.com, which was acquired by Yahoo in 1999 for $5.7 billion in Yahoo stock. Cuban took his passion for listening to Indiana Hoosier games and turned it into a multi-billion-dollar business.

Cuban was able to sell broadcast.com for a higher value due to being caught in the dotcom bubble. But his story isn't unique. Bubbles come and go in various industries every few years. You just have to have the eye to notice it and take advantage of it like Cuban did. Just like Cuban you too can turn almost any passion of yours into a multimillion, if not multibillion, dollar company. You just have to chase your dreams, not money.

Mark Cuban's story is not unique. Since I've graduated from college myself, I've realized something remarkable: almost all of today's most successful people were never *just* college students; they were always up to something else. They had grit and hustle.

The ordinary path is a cascading series of steppingstones, each marginally preparing you for the next. High school transitions you to college, and college transitions most of us to a corporate job. These institutions teach you to focus on earning good grades, avoiding distractions, following a set schedule, not working while in school unless you absolutely have to, and to focus focus focus. If you manage to graduate with a 9-5 job lined up post-ceremony, you're considered a winner. Meanwhile, entrepreneurship or freelancing are seldom considered real jobs because it can be harder to earn a steady paycheck which many fresh graduates may need. However, those who have the option to continue living at home with their parents will have lesser expenses, and as a result, will be at a slight advantage over others.

Two roads diverged in a wood, and I—
I took the one less traveled by,
And that has made all the difference.
Robert Frost

Entrepreneurship is the road less traveled; higher risk certainly, but with the potential to be more rewarding. And the road to entrepreneurship can begin during one's undergraduate years.

A college degree proves that you gained knowledge in a certain area, but it does not always translate to an ability to handle real-world problems that can't be taught in the classroom. One way—in addition to internships and other work experiences—that you can effectively learn how to deal with real-world issues is by thrusting yourself into those situations early. Firsthand experience is invaluable. Many successful people go after these experiences by doing something else substantial while they are college students.

When I was a full-time college student, most of time when I was not in class, doing homework, or at an internship, I spent running my own film festival. My tasks included advertising for film submissions, pre-screening and selecting from submitted films, negotiating with venues, scheduling films, and handling advertising and publicity to attract audiences. I started my film festival because I have a passion for film, but also because I wanted to do something that would make me stand out. (I am still running my film festival today on an annual basis. Though, the work for it is year-round.)

If you're fortunate, you will be able to attend college full-time and not also need to earn a paycheck. Grades are important, especially in the STEM (Science Technology Engineering and Math) fields. Going into the arts or starting your own business have less emphasis on grades, but all hiring managers look for more than just a good GPA. Even if you do need to work throughout college, there may be other ways to stand out, perhaps by starting a low-key but interesting side hustle. We'll explore that in future chapters, along with ways to balance school, work, and a side hustle without getting stressed, overwhelmed, or burnt out.

We have much to learn too, from others who have launched their successes by nurturing their entrepreneurial urges while still students. I'll introduce you to some others in the pages that follow. This book is your guide to how you too can be more than just a college student, and why it is now more important than ever to do just that—to create and build your own plus.

This book is for high school students who are thinking ahead, current college students, and recent graduates, some of whom may be early stage entrepreneurs. We'll be covering some big issues as well as how seemingly smaller things, like nailing down a daily routine, can contribute to your personal and career success, while in college and beyond.

The people you'll learn about here have figured out how to do their own thing and be their own boss. Some created their own steady source of income before taking a 9-5 job while others were able to grow their own source of income on the side and eventually quit their day jobs. You will even hear the story of someone who was able to arrange their life in a way that they get to take one month off every few months.

You may find one section or chapter useful now and another section useful at a slightly later stage in life. Take time between chapters so you can absorb the information and think about how you might apply the tips and strategies in your own life. You can revisit parts of the book every time you feel your life shifting course and need some new ideas. There's almost always a way to move in a new direction, if you're armed with your own unique plus

Chapter 1 – Mastering Time Your Way

Jack Dorsey is CEO of not one but *two* huge companies that most people use quite often: Square and Twitter. Square is a payments processing company popular with many small businesses, and Twitter is the popular social media platform where people publicly share thoughts in 280 characters or less. If you're like me, you're wondering, how on earth does Dorsey manage two enormous companies when I can barely manage one job?

**

We all have 24 hours in a day. Nobody has more, and nobody has less. Yet, it seems that some people can get more out of those 24 hours than others. Given that we have far less than 24 hours to spend on our work (one must sleep, eat, do chores, and socialize, after all), how can you structure your day and make sure you're spending the right amount of time on each task?

Mastering time management boils down to finding the most effective way to utilize your time. This usually involves planning out your day the night before or first thing in the morning, so you're ready to hit the ground running. It's different from multitasking. Time management is learning how to effectively allocate a set amount of time while multitasking is learning how to juggle a lot of tasks at the same time. (We'll discuss more about multitasking in Chapter Two.)

**

In an interview with Techonomy, Dorsey explained his secret to being productive for both companies while still working just eight hours a day. Dorsey said, "The way I found that works for me is I theme my days. On Monday, at both companies, I focus on management and running the company. Tuesdays is focused on product. Wednesday is focused on marketing and communications and growth. Thursday is focused on developers and partnerships. Friday is focused on the company and the culture and recruiting. Saturday, I take off, I hike. Sunday is reflection, feedback, strategy, and getting ready for the week."

Having a daily theme establishes a pattern. Because Dorsey focuses on a different section every day, those teams know they have a week between his follow-ups with them. Daily themes are also super useful because grouping similar tasks together has been proven to be quite efficient.

Even Steve Jobs, founder of Apple, was known for scheduling executive team meetings on Mondays, designating Wednesdays for advertising and marketing, and reserving most afternoons for design visits to Jony Ive, Apple's Chief Design Officer at the time.

How do the working habits of Jack Dorsey or Steve Jobs relate to the habits of a college student? After all, you probably don't have big teams working for you like top CEO's do. These CEO's break up their days of the week based on which part of their business they want to focus on each day of week. Which team they want to focus on. Similarly, you can substitute your classes and extracurricular activities for the parts of the business. Schedule out your days of the week and times of the day to focus on homework and studying for particular classes. Make sure to also incorporate club meetings into your weekly schedule as well since clubs will typically meet at the same time each week.

**

In order to plan your day effectively, start by making a list of everything that you have to or want to accomplish during that day. Essentially, you're trying to figure out how you can spend your 24 hours as effectively as possible. First, you need to understand how much time you'll need to spend on each task. Once you know that, get planning.

Master Time Management: Begin with a List

- Either the night before or the morning of, write down everything you want to accomplish that day.

- Keep it realistic. If you write down too many tasks, you'll overwhelm yourself.

- Allot time first for required activities—classes, homework, part time job.

- Don't over-schedule yourself and forget to budget time for sleeping, meals, household chores, family obligations. Everybody needs a different amount of sleep to function properly. Learn know how many hours work for you. Perhaps you will slot in naps throughout the day.

- Consider planning an entire week in one sitting. Looking at the longer-range picture may help you apportion tasks throughout the week to reach certain goals. Jack Dorsey creates a weekly plan for himself every Sunday.

- Think about whether to assign certain types of tasks to particular days, like Dorsey does.

- Whichever planning method you choose, record your daily to-do list in a way that feels most intuitive, a way you like. That may be on paper, in your phone, on your computer home page, in an app. Or, a combination of two of those.

- Then—most important of all—to stay on track, be sure to refer to your daily plan every morning, at least once during the day, and then again when you're nearing the end of the day.

Prioritizing the Daily List

How do you prioritize to-do items and figure out which ones to spend more time on?

First, determine how long it will likely take you to complete a task and then slot in that much time plus a buffer. If you think a task takes two hours, budget two hours and fifteen minutes so you have a little flexibility. Any buffer time you give yourself between tasks that isn't actually needed can be used as free time, to take a breather, or put toward another task that might be taking longer to complete than you had initially estimated.

Get the things that are the most difficult or take the most time done first. Mark Twain once said, "If it's your job to eat a frog, it's best to do it first thing in the morning. And if it's your job to eat two frogs, it's best to eat the biggest one first." If you do the most unbearable tasks, like eating a frog, first thing in the morning, you get them over with quickly, and taking on the hardest tasks early, like eating the bigger of the two frogs, will make subsequent tasks seem much smaller and easier to accomplish. This advice can be useful for both students and working professionals. Both groups need to know the most effective way to manage time and prioritize tasks.

Once you put things on your task list, give priority to them; do them because you know you *should* do them—even when something more tempting comes along. While it's important to have some flexibility, be wary of other opportunities that may sneak up and vie for your attention. Know what's urgent and what simply seems so. Sure, you can sometimes rearrange your schedule to take advantage of some hugely appealing last-minute outing with friends ("Hey, we have an extra ticket for XXX concert!), but more often, when it's something less dramatic ("Want to hang out and get a pizza?"), you'll need to ask yourself, "Do I have time for that, or will I just get behind?" Think about things that urgently need to get done versus things that are more of an impulse and may are not necessary. A sign of maturity is being able to say no; delaying gratification until a future moment when you can indulge without jeopardizing the important goals you put on your list. Staying on track is challenging, but do-able.

When you first decide to start managing your time in a meaningful way each day, you may have setbacks. Perhaps in the beginning you won't be budgeting your time well, or may not understand which tasks are priorities and which aren't. But if you keep with it, you can fine tune your daily to-do list until you ultimately land on a schedule that works for you. Even so, try to keep at least a part of your schedule flexible as the circumstances of your life can change at a moment's notice. You could have an unexpected family emergency, get fired from your job, or a task could simply just not go as you expected.

Having a "Plan B" is always a wise move. That way, when something unexpected yet urgent comes up, it won't throw your whole schedule off course. Instead, stop and think: how can I accomplish the necessary tasks of the day and also deal with this curveball? Deal with the interruption, and then put together a new schedule for the rest of your day afterward. Maybe something has to get jettisoned to tomorrow, or you can ask for help. Understand that you may not always accomplish everything you hoped to accomplish that day. That's okay. Life can be unpredictable sometimes.

Mastering Time for Meals

We all need to eat. Recognize that at least some of your time must be spent on getting groceries, preparing and cooking meals, and cleaning up. Even if you currently eat many of your meals in a dining hall, or at home prepared by someone else, at some point you will "graduate" to being responsible for feeding yourself! Eating good meals regularly is necessary for the brain and body, providing needed fuel for chasing after goals.

A system call "meal prep" has become popular with many young people. This involves setting aside a few hours, usually over the weekend, getting many well-balanced meals ready to go, in individual storage containers, saving time later in the week. Eating three meals per day, consisting of sound nutritional choices will keep you sharp and in good health. It's easy to get consumed by your work and not even realize that you've skipped a meal. When you have meals ready to go, you won't be tempted to skip meals or substitute unhealthy fast food options.

Meal prep is exactly what it sounds like: you are preparing many meals (usually dinners, but can also include lunches and breakfasts) all at once that will be ready to grab, cook, or heat up later, so that you will have enough easily accessible meals to give you a good balance of nutrition and energy.

Meal prep can also help you save money by buying grocery store ingredients in bulk and planning meals around what may be on sale. Even if you don't want a lot of hot foods or large meals, consider that buying a pre-made salad every day from a deli or restaurant is far more expensive than loading up on lettuce and other salad ingredients in the grocery store and making your own salads.

There are a number of websites and apps (like Mealime, Paprika, and PlateJoy) devoted to meal prep, where you can find recipes and tips, and learn which foods work best because they can last all week in the fridge, and which ones are not great candidates for meal prep. Cooked meat, roasted vegetables, soups, sauces, nuts, and stiff raw vegetables make good bases for meal prep recipes. Soft vegetables, cut fruit, and crunchy foods are a less than ideal choice because they quickly get soft in your refrigerator. Think about the salad I mentioned above. You could prep the lettuce base and items like cut up carrots, celery, and cucumbers over the weekend and add things like tomatoes, croutons, and salad dressing just before you eat. You can also buy precut veggies, easing yourself into meal prep, and see how this habit grows over time.

When using meal prep to assemble dinners that will be cooked later, be sure to take into account what you have available for cooking or heating. Do you have a stovetop? Oven? Microwave? Instapot? Or perhaps you can only do prepped cold meals for now—still a better option than restaurant prices or fast-food empty calories.

With meal prep, remember food safety. Use the best containers you can afford so food remains fresh as long as possible. Know how long the ingredients with usually last (those apps will tell you). Most devotees of meal prep set up about 3-5 days of meals at a time (though it may be possible, through a bit of trial and error, to find some longer lasting meals). Or consider making even more portions and freezing meals for future weeks.

Some meal prep folks like eating the same thing every day because it saves time; others like keeping the base the same (grilled chicken breasts, for example) while varying the vegetables or sauces. At first meal prep may take up a good chunk of a weekend day, but with practice, you'll get quicker at it and save time in the longer run.

Nobody knows how much food you need eat except you. Make sure each meal is portioned so you have enough food to fill yourself up, but not so much that you find yourself wasting food. Also make sure to account as best as you can for work lunches, happy hours, and times you are going out to eat with friends or family.

Even if you don't opt to do meal prep on a regular basis, be sure to set aside time in your weekly schedule for getting and cooking your own meals, snacks, and—if you're lucky enough—the time to eat out with family or friends.

Time for You: Personal Maintenance

Everyone has a body and mind that needs proper maintenance and attention in order for you to properly focus on your school or career tasks. Scheduling time for personal maintenance means thinking about things like doctor appointments, haircuts, working out, and other self-care tasks, and including them on daily to-do lists, rather than leaving them to chance.

Also, slot in occasional time for socializing and fun activities that will keep you sane. If you don't take care of yourself, you probably won't be good at taking care of your studies or work. Social outings, group functions, concerts, traveling (for pleasure), all contribute to your well-being. Remember the story of Square and Twitter CEO Jack Dorsey from earlier in the chapter? He runs three to five miles every morning. (More on morning routines in Chapter Three.)

Goals related to personal development fall into this category too. Perhaps you want to get more proficient at playing guitar, or one of your goals may be reading a new book each week. Look at your time commitments and find a way to schedule perhaps 20 minutes every day for music practice or reading, and setting reminders in your daily checklist, much as you would for a meeting. Some people find it beneficial to work toward their personal life goals at the same time every day while others may prefer turning to those pursuits at more random times when they need that boost in their day.

What's My Plus?

While in college—not right away, but eventually—I developed the ability to effectively manage my time, recognize and set priorities, and learn as much as I could from each job.

Fall semester during freshman year of college taught me my first real lesson about time management. In high school, I was so used to a schedule imposed upon me: seven hours of class daily followed by homework that was dur the next day, and only the occasional longer-term project. But once in college, with a very different daily class schedule, I had a lot more "free" time. With many larger assignments due late in the semester, I just pushed those off until…later. However, when later came and it was getting closer to the end of the semester, I realized I had a lot of work to do, and it was overwhelming me and stressing me out. I had wasted so much time earlier in the semester that I should have used to work on these big long-term assignments. I knew that going forward I was going to need to plan better, to more effectively use my time as I went along, and not save these big assignments until the end.

A few months later, during spring semester freshman year, I took a job with a company called Vector Marketing selling Cutco brand knives and other kitchen products. This was my first job and I had to make my own schedule, fitting in work hours whenever possible. Since this was a work when you want kind of job, the pay was only commission based. Meaning, it's a great job if you're really disciplined with your schedule and if you're good at sales. While this might sound ideal, it boiled down to only working when I wanted to work—and let's be honest, for a college student who didn't need the income, that meant not working much at all. And if you're not good at sales or time management, you won't make very much money. As a result, after a few weeks, I found myself having poor time management, spending most of the time outside of class lazing around and wasting time. The only advantage was that once I noticed this tendency, I realized I needed to start creating a schedule for myself.

I started by blocking out the times I was in class. Next, I estimated how much time I would need daily for homework so I could put that in my schedule as well. Next, I set a goal for myself of how many sales presentations I wanted to do per week in order to make a certain amount of money. This system proved to work well for me and I created a regular pattern of working hours, learning a lot along the way about confidence, how to talk to consumers, and how to close a sale.

A while after I left that job, I got a summer job through a third-party company, selling TV, phone, and internet for Verizon. This was much more regimented, with regular hours, management supervision, and quotas. The company had a schedule pre-planned for each employee, which I found very helpful. I worked six days per week. Each day, we spent time learning or practicing sales techniques and getting our scripts memorized. Then, we would go out in the field, with a route mapped out so we could hit about sixty houses. I found that having this structure laid out for me worked much better for me than the Vector Marketing job which frankly offered me too much freedom at that time in my early working life, when I was still rather disorganized.

Those early working experiences taught me a lot, and since then I have learned how to be more organized and in control of my time and life.

Chapter 1 Takeaways

1. Make a list of tasks you need or want to accomplish each day.

2. Prioritize tasks according to importance.

3. Estimate how long each task will take you to complete and allow some buffer time.

4. Adjust schedule as needed to address unexpected developments and disruptions.

5. Attend to your nutritional health. Consider trying meal prep.

6. Remember to take care of your personal needs.

7. Recognize the need to be mature and judicious in weighing time-stealing "appealing" options.

Chapter 2 – Multitasking, a Myth

Many people think that multitasking is the answer to time management. Multitasking means dealing with several different task at the same time—multiple homework assignments, multiple projects for school or work, or even a lot of household chores. By multitasking, we believe we can effectively get all the tasks done in a compressed timeframe without neglecting any of them.

However, multitasking is misunderstood. Those who study the brain tell us that multitasking really doesn't even exist, that when we think we are multitasking, we are simply switching very rapidly from one task to another and back again. This may be useful on occasion, but most of the time, we achieve peak performance when we avoid multitasking. Multitasking splits your focus between multiple tasks at once, and this makes it easy to mix up tasks, hurry and make mistakes, or neglect necessary parts of a task. If you've properly planned your day (discussed in the previous chapter), you've allotted enough time for each individual task and multitasking won't be necessary.

There's really no such thing as multitasking well. Cognitive psychologist Art Markman says, "The human brain doesn't really multitask. What the human brain does is what I call time-sharing. With time-sharing, your brain can only think about one task at a time, so you focus on that one task. After, another takes its place. Your brain shifts between tasks so fast that you don't even realize that you're actually only doing one task at a time. You feel like you're multitasking, but you are actually time-sharing."

Most people assume that they are good at multitasking, but they're really just deceiving themselves. Markman says, "You are your own worst judge of how good a multitasker you are." The areas of your brain which monitor performance are the same areas which are used in multitasking, so when multitasking, your brain has less bandwidth available to properly evaluate your own performance. You think you are performing better than you actually are.

True multitasking divides your brainpower. Yet, some busy, high-powered people get close to achieving a state that mimics multitasking because their brains work differently than the rest of us. For most of us, the parts of our brain associated with performing multiple tasks at once overheat when we try to multitask; those who have the gift of being able to truly multitask are referred to as "super multitaskers." These people have a higher neural efficiency which allows their brain to remain cool while performing multiple tasks at once. Since most people can't actually multitask, performing multiple tasks very quickly in a row has become known commonly known as multitasking – so that's how I'll use the term for the rest of this chapter.

This more common reference to multitasking—moving from one task to another and back again—is helpful when you must juggle several tasks that will either take a long time, or have long-range deadlines. When you need a break from working on a longer project, you can switch to another, knocking off chunks of each while making steady progress on both.

Even if you are good at time sharing—what we refer to as multitasking—planning your day remains paramount, as does prioritizing tasks based on urgency—or else you won't know when to multitask, and which projects to flip back and forth between. Planning your day and multitasking go hand in hand because effective planning of your day can allow you to minimize the amount of multitasking needed to get all your tasks completed.

What about when multitasking seems absolutely necessary, like when tasks overlap one another because of conflicting deadlines, imposed expectations, or a time crunch brought on by an unexpected disruption? We don't even need a school or workplace scenario to illustrate this; everyday life offers its own versions.

Imagine you're getting ready to host friends for dinner. You're making a series of courses that each need minimal supervision after the initial prep. You go about putting together appetizers, tidying up, or setting the table while also periodically checking in on the chicken that's roasting, the soup that's simmering, the garlic bread that's toasting. This is a much better utilization of your time than standing in front of the stove staring at a pot that doesn't require constant stirring. You get more work done in the time before your guests arrive by staying in motion, rapidly moving between several tasks, while others have been set in motion in the background.

When working on several things in the same time period, your mind still needs to rest, so it may help to change the medium of the task you are working on. Take a break from math homework and do some chores like vacuuming or taking out the trash. When writing that work report, try switching between reading and writing, or add in an audio or visual item from elsewhere on your to-do list, or something physical that needs doing. This way, you get your break but you still get some other work item done, and return to the original task refreshed. This will help you avoid concentration burn-out and enhance performance.

Whether you call it multitasking, or time sharing, or just "getting a lot done at once," it's important to learn how to do so efficiently, to find a way that works for you when faced with multiple demands. But it's equally as important to know the reality of false multitasking, and that your more complicated tasks call for complete focus, not a scattershot approach. Save the multitasking for more mundane tasks or those you are used to performing regularly and almost feel like you could complete in your sleep.

Juan Acosta

I met Juan Acosta in the summer of 2016 at the Draper University program for entrepreneurs in Silicon Valley, where he was Entrepreneur-in-Residence, making himself available to attendees, and guiding us, much like a resident advisor in a college dormitory.

Before working at Draper University, Juan was a student of the program, and before that, Juan's full-time job was working for the largest Latin American video game distributor. At the same time, he was running a web agency as his side hustle because Juan always had ambitions to make a living on his own terms.

Juan recommends combining your passions whenever you can. If you have one job but are also trying to build another (via a side hustle), don't choose ones that are completely unrelated to each other. Everything you are working on should all be part of a larger singular goal or vision you have for yourself. For Juan, that goal is to help startups and entrepreneurs through struggles similar to the ones he's faced in the past and continues to face today.

Juan was not Entrepreneur-in-Residence at Draper University for long, but quickly rose in ranks and began working on the fund which Draper University established to invest in companies started by alumni of their program. He was able to rise quickly due to the way he was able to understand and connect with the entrepreneurs who attended the program since he can relate to their struggles on a personal level since he was there himself not so long ago. Juan also had several side hustles going, which he would work on during his spare time at Draper University. These tied in directly with his goal of helping startups and entrepreneurs.

Juan is currently working on a mental health project, aiming to understand how entrepreneurship affects the mental health of founders. He chose this project after noticing how entrepreneurs are so often stressed and overworked, leading to isolation and a pursuit of perfection which can breed depression, loneliness, and a feeling of inadequacy. Juan wanted to see if there was a common factor and if there was anything he could do to help entrepreneurs manage these emotions.

Juan describes the central goal or vision that everyone should have as their "northern star," guiding them on the journey that is their life. He finds that having all his projects overlapping in some capacity allows for peak efficiency, and eliminates much of the need for multitasking. Much of the research needed for one of his projects can be useful for his other projects. The similarity in the nature of his projects allows him to take on more projects without dramatically increasing the amount of prep work. Juan believes that everyone needs that unified northern star vision in order to be as successful as they can be in their life.

What's My Plus?

While in college, it's often difficult to avoid having a lot of things going on at the same time—classes, studying, internships, part time job, social life, all while trying to graduate on time. To manage it all, there were many times when I needed to work more efficiently, to multitask, or time share. I wasn't successful at this every semester, but I learned.

I wanted to graduate in four years, so I had kept myself pretty well on track by taking the requisite number of credits each semester. Usually that meant registering for five classes three-credit courses each semester, which is a reasonable load. But some semesters didn't work out that way—a result of my not paying enough attention to the prerequisites and required courses in my major, and letting too many 4-credit courses accumulate, until I had no choice but to endure a few semesters with a much heavier semester credit load. One semester, I was taking seventeen credits, and had also signed up for an online course through the Massachusetts Institute of Technology.

Although this class was a certification class and not a credited class towards my degree, it was still like another three-credit class which was completely online, so it felt like I was taking twenty credits total that semester.

During this intense semester, I was spending all my time outside of the classroom working on assignments. I found it very hard to juggle all the work, was trying my best to multitask, but could feel my brain getting overheated. I felt as if I didn't have time to take breaks for activities not related to homework, and relied on multitasking (time sharing), constantly switching between assignments for different classes, but never taking a break. While this never felt great, in the end, I believe the only thing that got me through that semester was moving between tasks and not getting stuck. This may not have been ideal, but when faced with conflicting, overlapping demands, I learned the value of letting my brain focus shift between different projects.

Another tough semester was my final semester, during the spring of 2019. I had a lot going on, but it felt entirely different because the demands weren't all school work. Yes, I was taking a regular load of five three-credit classes, but I also had a part time internship three days per week, and I was working on the Visionaries Film Festival, which I had started the previous year. Everything was connected to my "northern star" vision—overlapping projects that all represented different aspects of the same basic life/work interests.

This time, I was able to put into action some of what I'd learned from Juan Acosta. Research for the film festival also contributed to some of my course work assignments and vice versa. At my internship, I was learning and doing things that helped me develop a better plan for what the film festival needed, and enhanced my understanding of what my professors were teaching in my major courses.

While my internship didn't require much work outside of the hours I was actually at the studio, and I was already skilled at keeping on top of my assignments for my classes, the film festival posed challenges. Because I was the only one keeping myself accountable for that project, I found that I was neglecting some of the necessary work to make it grow, and instead, intuitively prioritized time for school assignments, which of course made sense: graduating on time was an important goal. I was doing my best to multitask, but often flailing around, wasting time, and failing to move ahead on all fronts. I learned that multitasking won't work when you understand deep down that one task must take precedence. And I learned that I should have been creating a schedule, every day (discussed in Chapter One), and then prioritizing tasks, and budgeting my time accordingly.

Chapter 2 Takeaways

1. True multitasking is mostly a myth.

2. While some folks can truly multitask; most of us "time share," working on tasks in rapid rotation.

3. Try to avoid the need for multitasking if possible by creating a schedule and prioritizing tasks and goals.

4. It is easy to make careless mistakes on work when trying to multitask.

5. Rotating tasks and switching back and forth between projects works when you have a large amount of work to be completed in the same short amount of time.

6. When your jobs, side hustle, and passion projects are closely related, you can more efficiently and "multitask," as some areas will overlap.

Chapter 3 – Mastering Morning Routines

Getting your day started off right pays dividends. Having a morning routine is a crucial part of being successful in college or the work world, and any successful person you admire will tell you just that. A morning routine gives you time to focus on yourself and leads to a more productive day overall. Most, if not all, of your favorite celebrities have a morning routine. Some people stick to a stricter morning routine than others. Much depends on how self-disciplined the person is, how their days are typically structured, what demands and obligations must usually be met, and the degree to which flexibility is a factor.

Celebrity Morning Routines

Mark Zuckerberg, CEO of Facebook, wears the same outfit every day so that he has one less decision he needs to make. This allows him to free up the time he would have spent choosing an outfit for more important tasks. Tim Cook, CEO of Apple, checks his email when he wakes up every morning and then goes to exercise. Exercising in the morning leads to lower stress levels, a better mood overall for your day, and higher energy levels.

Richard Branson, founder of the Virgin Group, and Jeff Bezos, CEO of Amazon, both make time for family each morning. Even president Obama would help his daughters get ready for school in the morning while he was president. If CEOs and world leaders can make time for their family in the morning, you can too. This can be parents, siblings, or even pets. If you don't live with your family, you can substitute family time for time with your roommate(s).

Arianna Huffington, founder of the Huffington Post and Thrive Global, starts her days off with yoga, meditation, and setting her intention for the day. It is important to set an intention each morning, so you have a clear focus on what you want to achieve that day and don't get bogged down or overwhelmed. Your intention for the day is a central theme which all your tasks for that day revolve around.

Mindfulness Daily is a free app that helps you build a daily mindfulness routine. The app recommends you start your day by taking a few moments to set your intention for the day before getting started with your day. This will help you begin your day with clarity. Then, the app recommends that you take a quick moment to pause and collect yourself when you feel stressed. Finally, the app recommends thar you take a few moments at the end of your day to unwind and reflect on your day. It's a good idea to use an app like Mindfulness Daily to remind you to be mindful and to set intentions throughout your day until it becomes so ingrained in you that you begin to do it automatically.

Morning Routines for Everyone

While you can find the morning routine for most well-known people somewhere online, creating your own routine is what matters. Having a steady morning routine leads to a more successful and more productive day. While some morning routine includes waking up early—science tell us that people tend to be more productive early in the morning than late at night—that may not necessarily be true for you and your body clock. As you read, remember that "morning" can mean different times to different people. A routine is simply something that you do right after you wake up, whether that's two in the morning like Mark Wahlberg, or 10 a.m.

People who wake up earlier are not necessarily more productive. Rather, people who are more productive tend to wake up earlier in the morning, or perhaps simply earlier than they strictly need to, building in extra time in their day before they must report to work or class. The more productive folks tend to have a set morning routine, building in extra time, while those who wake up later and have less time before they must get to work usually don't have a set routine.

In order to wake up early enough to have an unrushed morning routine, ensure that you go to bed at a reasonable time so you sleep for an adequate number of hours. The amount of sleep everyone needs varies from person to person. Sleep experts advise that the best way to ensure you fall asleep quickly, stay asleep throughout the night, and wake up feeling refreshed is to go to sleep and wake up around the same time each day. Also, it is recommended to not do anything in bed except sleeping—no eating in bed, watching television in bed, or using your phone. If you are using screens at night, use a blue light filter so you don't mess with the natural sleep indicators your brain would otherwise send out to your body. Most modern smartphones come with a built-in blue light filter. I have mine set so that it automatically goes on each night and off each morning at the same times.

Other than washing up, getting dressed, and having a healthy breakfast, what should you add to your morning routine so you can be the most productive? The answer will be different for everyone. Take small steps as you build your routine. Here are some examples of things common to successful morning routines:

Breakfast

The simplest thing you can do for your morning routine is to have a healthy and wholesome breakfast. Many people forget to factor breakfast time into their mornings and either skip it or end up eating some sort of unhealthy grab-and-go breakfast like toaster pastries or granola bars which often both contain high amounts of sugar. Having a healthy balanced breakfast gives you the energy to tackle all your tasks for that day head on. You might even find you enjoy preparing the meal, and perhaps looking over the news of the day while you eat.

Self-care

Budget time for grooming each morning. Put that trimmer or electric toothbrush you will need the next morning on the charger the night before. Make sure your clothes are clean and ironed. Allot time for washing up, make-up, hair styling. If you are going to attend an important meeting or make a presentation, you might want to pick out your outfit the night before. Running out the door without eating, with your hair in disarray, or feeling rushed can mean a bad start to your day, putting you in in a foul mood.

Exercise

Some people find exercise to be a great start to their day. This can consist of anything from yoga to running to a full workout. Putting a workout into your morning schedule gets your blood flowing and energizes you, as well as contributing to overall good health and weight management. For some people, exercise is the toughest thing, and they will likely put it off all day, but if you "eat the frog" first thing in the morning, you will feel accomplished early on. Once you get to the point where you're exercising without really thinking about it, you'll be able to go through the routine without using much mental energy. Exercise can give you a similar boost to caffeine but in a natural way.

Meditation/Prayer

Meditation or prayer is another great way to begin your day. If you observe an organized religion or faith tradition, learn which prayers are recommended, and that you like, for morning. Calm and guided meditation is so much easier than in the past, with apps like Headspace, which include different sounds and moods depending on what kind of day you want to have. Now, there's even a new type of virtual church that seems to be engaging with younger adults in their 20s and 30s to stay connected with their faith without having to get up and drive to a place of worship early in the morning. One example is Life.Church, which is the largest online church service.

Family Time

Spending time to spend with family in the morning can be a nice boost. If you live with parents, siblings, a spouse/mate, grandparents, some morning conversation, perhaps over breakfast, can be a nice reminder that you are part of a loving group. Time with roommates also falls into this category. And if you live on your own, you might consider catching up with distant relatives over Skype or Facetime for a few minutes while you start your day.

Let's not forget about family pets. A morning routine might need to include some feeding or grooming time. A lot of people take their dogs on morning walks, or along for a morning run. Just a few minutes playing with your pets, cuddling with them, or showing them affection will increase your sense of wellbeing at the start of your day.

Hobbies

Mornings are also a great time to practice your passions and connect with art or craft pursuits. This could be anything from painting, to playing an instrument, reading a magazine, watering plants. Consider getting up early enough to schedule time to practice and perfect your craft each morning. Start your day with a jolt of inspiration from doing what you love – not what you're told to do.

Household Chores

Most people don't love cleaning, tidying up, or other household chores—but we all agree they must be done if we want to live in a nice environment. Including even just 10 minutes of household chores in your morning routine might make sense, and lessen the load later in the day when you're returned home tired. If you take out the trash, empty the dishwasher, make your bed in the morning, you'll return to a calmer, cleaner home later on.

Schedules

Your morning is the ideal time for scheduling your day. Prioritize tasks in a to-do list and plan out your day. (Review the topics discussed in Chapter One about time management.). Take some time to sit down and say "this is what I want to accomplish today, and here's how I'll get it all done." If you made a list at the end of your day yesterday, start off by attacking those tasks first. Kenneth Chenault, the former CEO of American Express used to end every work day with a list of the three most important things he wanted to tackle the following day. He would start each morning by looking at the list he made the previous day.

Morning Sounds

Many people like to incorporate sounds into their morning routine. Some like to listen to music while they shower. Others get a morning boost by listening to upbeat music throughout their whole morning or on the way to work or school. These days, many people listen to podcasts as part of their morning routine for some morning motivation.

Getting into a routine

What goes into your morning routine will be different for everyone, so there's no one routine that will work for everyone. If there's something that you want to do as part of your routine, but the idea seems intimidating at first, ease yourself into it. If you want to work out, for example, but you aren't that fit, start with just 10 minutes of easy exercise and work your way up to a full workout. Try lifting five-pound weights, learning a handful of yoga poses, a dozen push-ups, walking a quarter-mile. Then add a new exercise or more time or distance every morning. Show up (or tune in) for a yoga class just 3 days per week instead of every day. Start small, and increase as you go. Don't bite off more than you can chew.

If you're not a "morning person," then an abbreviated routine will work best. Perhaps you will instead have an "end of day" routine in the evening before you go to bed—showering, creating your schedule, doing chores, or indulging in a hobby in the evening hours. The important thing is to make time in your day to take care of yourself so that when you do have to get to work or school, you arrive rested and feeling as if your day is off to a good start.

What's My Plus?

Before I had a set morning routine, I used to go to sleep at random times. As a result, I sometimes found it difficult to fall asleep. I also occasionally found myself waking up in the middle of the night and not being able to fall back asleep easily. When I had no set time for waking up, I would often wake up half asleep and groggy and without a routine, my mornings were often rushed and disorganized.

At some point I realized that I had to manage my routine during the week. (Weekends we all sometimes vary our sleep and daytime schedules.) During the week, I try to go to sleep between 11 PM and 11:30 PM. When I wake up in the morning, I start by checking my notifications and email on my phone so I find out any important news I might need to know as I plan my day. I decide whether to reply immediately to an email or wait depending on how long I expect it to take me. Next, I take care of grooming, getting dressed, and I always make sure I have enough time for breakfast. I have also made a habit of meditating before I go to sleep, and I am working towards regularly meditating first thing in the morning as well. Knowing I have a set routine helps me wake up more refreshed each morning, and going through my routine gets me mentally ready to take on the day.

Chapter 3 Takeaways

1. Everyone's morning routines are different. Get ideas from others, but create your own.

2. Go to sleep at a reasonable time to ensure you get a good night sleep.

3. Make time for a healthy breakfast.

4. Budget time for self-care.

5. Create or update your day's to-do list.

6. Consider incorporating meditation, prayer, sounds, family time, exercise.

Chapter 4 – School Life Balance

During college, every student has different circumstances, varying demands on their time, and a unique personal life. Some students may need to maintain a job so they can cover the cost of college or have spending money. Others may be tasked with picking up younger siblings after school. Other students may already be parents themselves, or be struggling with medical issues or complicated family circumstances.

Whatever it may be, it's quite possible that you may have something in your life which you need to plan your classes, studying, and work around. Sometimes, when the timing of a certain required class conflicts with your schedule, you may need to modify your personal life to fit with your class schedule for school—or, vice versa.

School life balance refers to how students balance schoolwork with everything going on in their lives. This includes the best way to structure your class schedule, what kind of job and how many working hours fits in best, meeting family or other obligations without neglecting school. The goal is to strike an optimal balance and not get overwhelmed.

Whether you are taking a full-time course load, or are a part-time student, you'll find useful tips in this chapter. (By the way, there are many reasons one might not be a full-time college student, so don't ever feel like you're going about college in the wrong way. Any road that gets you to a college degree can be right for you.)

Not everyone is lucky enough to have parents who can fully pay for college, or have their tuition mostly covered by scholarships and grants. Whether you are working while a student in order to pay tuition, to ease the burden on parents and have your own spending money, or to build up some savings for when the time comes to pay off student loans, achieving a good school life balance is necessary.

Personal Life

Students with a lot going on in their personal life may find it best to register for classes that meet less frequently than usual—once or twice a week instead of three time, for example. All–online or hybrid (combination online and in-person) classes are other options that may make a school life balance easier to attain.

If you live off campus, factor the commute into your schedule. See if you can minimize your commutes by planning your class schedule in a way that doesn't require you to travel back and forth to campus several times in a day. Avoid commuting at rush hour if possible. If living on or very close to campus is possible, you'll slash commuting time even more, freeing up more time for studying, sleeping, and socializing. Plus, you'll be able to go home between classes.

Downtime Between Classes

If you have a long stretch of downtime between classes, there are many options other than hanging about with friends—options that help you get more done. Obviously, you can go to the library to get some work done in a quiet environment. Most colleges also offer vast lobbies, commuter lounges, student centers, and other shared public spaces with comfortable seating, Wi-Fi connections, work tables, etc. Find places you can work and take advantage of what's available to catch up on required reading, homework, or school-related emails.

Check out the tutoring center if you are struggling in any of your classes. Visit professors during their office hours during if you need some extra help in their class. Most professors are accommodating and will usually schedule an alternate time to meet you if you cannot attend regular office hours.

A long stretch of downtime is also a good opportunity to check out activities of interest on campus or attend meetings of clubs that appeal to you. When you are an upper-class student, you can usually also try to plan your class schedule around meetings of any clubs you are interested in.

If you've been up late studying, a long break between classes is a great time to take a nap. All those places mentioned above usually offer couches and quiet corners, sometimes even entire rooms designated for quiet and kept on the darker side. Most universities also have a grassy quad which is a great place to relax when the weather is nice. If there are trees, you might even be able to set up a hammock!

Some colleges offer free classes in the computer lab or library which teach various skills, a great way to continue learning during your downtime. Every college also has a career services department which can help you find on-campus jobs, off-campus jobs, internships, and co-ops.

When you are nearing graduation, stop in often for help with interview skills, resume writing, and cover letters. You'll also find information there about upcoming job fairs and on-campus recruiting; sure, it's all on the website, but an in-person relationship with a career counselor might give you an edge and let you ask questions face to face.

Homework

Of course, as a college student, you'll want to work on your homework whenever and wherever you can. It helps to have a running list of all your assignments and due dates on a digital calendar. Use the calendar app that comes built into your phones and laptop or use Google Calendar to set notifications that will ensure you don't miss any deadlines, and so that you can see at a glance which assignments are due next.

The first week of the semester is always known, either officially or unofficially, as "syllabus week," when professors hand out the syllabus for their class and go over their expectations and assignments for the semester. Don't skip those initial classes! Use the syllabi to add due dates for projects, essays, and exam dates to your digital calendar. Note which professors mention that the syllabus may change throughout the semester so that you can keep alert for these changes and adjust your digital calendar as needed.

Some professors set up a steady stream of assignment deadlines throughout the semester. Other professors list only a few assignments for early in the semester but assign a few much larger projects due later in the semester. In this case, it is a good idea to give yourself mini-goals throughout your semester to avoid getting overwhelmed and unnecessarily stressed as the due dates pile up near the end of the semester. If you utilize small blocks of time steadily throughout the entire semester to get a jump start on long-range assignments, you can lessen your stress and stay in balance.

In an Intro to Poetry class I took, the long-range assignment was to write reactions to 30 poems. We had to keep a running journal though nothing was due until the end. I decided to create mini-goals, picking three interim dates throughout the semester, figuring I needed to complete writing about 10 poems each time, so I would avoid the panic of writing about all 30 poems at the last minute.

Study Tips

Having a study buddy or being part of a study group pays off. You will keep each other accountable throughout the semester, and you'll always have someone who can help you if you're struggling. Study buddies or study groups can share study strategies and help get each other ready before exams, teaming up to share particular strengths, and ease the tedium of staring at a textbook all alone at your desk.

If you're taking an online course, try to take it with a friend so you can keep each other accountable. Also take advantage of online resources in places like Blackboard and Canvas, which usually make it easy to interact with other students and faculty, ask questions, and find all the materials for a course in one online spot.

Scheduling Your Semester

You can create the best school life balance if you have some flexibility in the way you choose and schedule your classes.

I had an opportunity to talk to a college student named Samir about the awesome way he manages a full college course load with his personal life. During one semester when Samir needed to take more than the average number of credits for a full-time student, while also working a sizable number of hours per week, he made sure to research his classes and professors beforehand. He picked up intel about which classes and professors were more demanding and which ones had less formidable expectations, and created a class schedule so that he had a good balance of each. Samir wanted to make sure the semester wasn't going to be too easy or too hard, keeping it in balance with the amount of time he'd have available for studying and homework, and his job. This way, he didn't overwork himself yet still could get good grades, maintaining his GPA. Your GPA is like a credit score: easier to maintain a good one than to fix a bad one.

It's tempting, early in your college career, to design a semester or two filled with easier courses, putting off harder courses for later. While this might help with personal life issues or allow more time for a job, it can backfire once you get closer to graduation and realize you are left with only the hardest courses for your major. A full semester or two of tough courses all at once is really hard for any student, and it can cause unneeded stress, lack of sleep, and lead to bad grades and a drop in GPA. It's a lot better to make your semesters balanced, spreading out the tough courses over the entirety of your college career. Samir knew this and made it a big part of how he decided which courses to take alongside his internship.

A smart strategy when planning your courses is to talk to students who are a year or two ahead of you in your program. They have experience with various courses and many professors, making them uniquely situated to advise you Of course, your official college advisors are always there for you, and you should tap their brains too. They are trained to help you, your tuition dollars are paying for this "free" service, and they often have a written plan for the best way to plan out your semesters so they are all well balanced.

What's My Plus?

Early in my college career, I was guilty of taking a semester or two full of mostly lightweight courses. I thought I was being smart and almost gaming the system, but all I was doing was putting off my hard courses. Eventually, I had one semester where I had no choice but to take a bunch of tough courses, totaling about 20 credits. I was spending literally all my time outside the classroom—weekdays as well as nights and weekends—doing homework, studying, and working on projects. During that semester, I had to say no almost every time someone asked me to hang out.

While I was learning that lesson, I also figured out the importance of allotting some time for non-classroom college activities—activities that would feed my passions, bring me in touch with others who shared my interests, and in the long run, also gain some useful skills.

At my school, Montclair State University, I discovered the Video Production Club—perfect for a student with my interests. Unfortunately, during the semester I learned about the club, I had a class at the same time as their weekly meetings. Yet I was still able to be involved with the club as much as I could outside of their meetings, working on events and supporting club activities. After that semester, I tried my best to structure semesters so that I had an open slot in my class schedule when the Video Production Club met.

Sometimes the only time you can fit a required class into your schedule will be at the same time a club you are a member of meets. Those who run clubs on a college campus understand this, and if you talk to the board members and let them know of your interest, they'll usually offer way you can still be involved.

For me, making time for the Video Production Club led me to eventually starting a film festival; paying attention to this particular part of the school life balance helped me develop a side hustle in an overlapping area of interest (shades of Juan Acosta!).

Chapter 4 Takeaways

1. It doesn't matter if you're a full-time or part-time student.

2. It's okay to not graduate college in four years.

3. Personal circumstances play a role. Work toward balance rather than fighting against them.

4. When planning which classes to take and when, consider personal obligations, commuting issues, GPA, and your program's requirements.

5. Make the most of your free time by tapping all your institution's resources.

6. Use a digital calendar to keep on top of deadlines.

7. Have a study buddy, or join or create a study group for each of your classes.

8. Talk to older students in your program and learn from their experiences.

Chapter 5 – Work Life Balance

Picture this. You're waking up at 6 AM for work and not getting home until twelve hours later. You're exhausted after a long day, and all you want is to throw a frozen dinner in the microwave, watch reruns of *Friends*, and go to sleep. You don't get time to do anything personal on workdays, and if you do get time, you just don't have the energy. As a result, you don't rest on your days off because you're busy taking care of your personal life. There has to be something you can do to better balance your work life with your personal life so your entire life isn't consumed by your job. It's too easy to get consumed by your job, especially a first job, and have your life pass by while you miss important moments with family and friends.

The above scenario may seem pretty crazy to you if you have never had a full-time job before. However, it is all too common. It is normal to work eight hours per day, and sometimes more in a full-time job. Add in the time it takes you to get ready in the morning and commute times of sometimes more than an hour. In total, it's not uncommon to be consumed by your job for 12 or 13 hours total each day. At first, this may be tough to get used to, or you may feel that a job with a less regimented schedule may be better for you.

Achieving a good work life balance is necessary when you have a full-time job as well as an active social or home life. Unlike with school life, a work life balance is trickier because you have much less flexibility with your schedule. While some jobs, especially freelance or contractor positions, have flexibility, most positions follow some semblance of a strict nine-to-five schedule that only allows for limited vacation, personal, and sick days.

Spending too much time on your work can lead to fatigue, poor health, lost time with friends and loved ones, and in some cases, increased expectations from your employer. Make sure you do a good job at your job, but don't overwork yourself. Give your job your 100% best effort, but don't take on more work than you can handle. In larger companies, you may get asked to work on various projects by people on several different teams. They are usually understanding if you tell them you already have more on your plate than you can handle. They honestly don't know if others have given you work, and they really just want to make sure you're being utilized and not sitting idly with nothing to do. Overworking will lead to you getting unnecessarily stressed, and it may even lead to burn out.

If you are being overworked, it is okay to tell your boss once in a while. However, you don't want to be telling this to your boss all the time or they will feel like you're trying to take advantage of their understanding nature. Instead of telling your boss that you feel like you're being overworked, try gently explaining to them that they've given you more work than you can complete by their respective deadlines. Bosses usually understand the consequences linked to employees being overworked and are willing to work with you. Most bosses aren't inherently bad people. Your boss is likely preoccupied with their own life stresses. They wants to create the optimal scenario for your success, as best as they can, because your success reflects well on them as a boss, and their success reflects well on the company as whole.

As you make your daily to-do list and prioritize and divide your time, try not to take on more tasks than you think you can manage in a day. If you absolutely have to, ask someone to assist you, delegate some of your tasks, or explain to your boss why you won't be able to get to certain tasks today. The only thing worse than telling someone you can't take on a task is to agree to complete it and then end up not having enough time to get it done.

Breaks

Remember to take breaks throughout the day at work. If your office has a break room or nap pods, make use of them when you can. If you work indoors all day, a break is a good opportunity to step outside and get some fresh air. If you work on your feet all day, find time to sit down and rest your feet. Sometimes that little change is just what you need to give you the energy to power through the rest of your workday.

When you begin working full-time, it's good idea to learn what laws in your state govern the workplace.

According to the Fair Labor Standards Act (FLSA), employers are not required to provide meal or breaks to employees. When employers do choose to provide employees with meal or rest breaks, restrictions apply. Breaks that are 20 minutes or less are required to be paid, and they count toward the total amount when calculating employee overtime. Breaks that are 30 minutes or longer are not required to be paid if the employee is relieved of all work duties.

Whether or not you are paid for your breaks, they help you keep a positive mental health. A lunch break is a great opportunity to get up from your desk, get fresh air and/or some exercise, refuel with some food, and clear your head. If you have time left after getting something to eat, take a walk; if your workplace provides a well-stocked break room, maybe you can do something like play a game of ping pong with a coworker.

Angie Carrillo

Angie Carrillo kept making changes throughout her professional life until she found a career path and lifestyle that works for her. Her story makes me think about how I want to live my life in the future. I hope her story will enlighten you in the same way which it enlightened me.

After attending a technologically geared college in Mexico, Angie began her career as a founder at two startups in the Ed-tech & Bio-tech fields. She was able to help those companies get into startup accelerators, and she even helped them secure funding from investors. Eventually, the work became too strenuous for Angie and she parted ways with those companies. She decided to take what she had learned during her time at those companies and use it to become a mentor to other startups and aspiring entrepreneurs.

The above photo is of Angie Carrillo

Yc   two, or even one, startups right out of college like Angie. However, you will get a full-time job where you will learn a lot of new things just like Angie, and you can then mentor others or become a consultant to use the knowledge you learn over a few years to teach people in similar situations like you.

Now, Angie assists entrepreneurs with business development and securing fundraising for their startups. She typically works with early stage startups seeking seed round investment, which is typically the first official fundraising round after friends and family and, of course, the founders' bootstrapping. Some of the companies Angie has worked with include one which made it into the Y Combinator program (one of the top startup accelerators in the U.S.), and got ranked in the top 30 by Forbes Magazine.

A solid work life balance is a must for Angie. She wanted to find a way to balance both her work life and her personal life as opposed to prioritizing one over the other. As an independent contractor, Angie typically works as a consultant with a client company for up to three months and then takes a one-month break. This is a strategy she learned by reading *The 4-Hour Workweek* by Tim Ferris. While this strategy may not seem extreme, it is what works best for Angie. (For more bold advice from Tim Ferris, look up his other books—which many entrepreneurs find helpful in shaping their career, mindset, and lifestyle—and his podcast, called The Tim Ferris Show, for interviews with other entrepreneurs.)

During Angie's one-month vacations, she uses her income from consulting to fund travels all over the world, documenting her experiences on Instagram (@angiecarrillor). Traveling is truly one of her passions, and she has gained an organic social media following as a result. As of August 2020, Angie had 23.3 thousand followers and counting, and she consistently gets between 1.5-3.5 thousand likes per post. To connect her passions for startup consulting and traveling, Angie helps founders from all over the world, whom she encounters on her travels, to tap into the Silicon Valley market.

Angie is very candid and honest about her experiences. Though she could become an influencer and monetize her Instagram account if she wanted to, she has chosen not to, keeping it as just a way to share photos from her vacations.

Besides doing what makes her happy for a living and taking one-month vacations, Angie has several other ways she is able to maintain a good work life balance. She makes it a point to exercise daily and to make sure she's drinking plenty of water so she stays properly hydrated. Angie has also been meditating for over 15 years, incorporating it as a daily habit. Some benefits of meditation include reduced stress, reduced anxiety, good positive mental health.

Angie is also a lover of positive psychology, which the University of Pennsylvania's Positive Psychology Center, defines as the scientific study of the strengths that enable individuals and communities to thrive. Positive psychology is founded on the belief that people want to lead meaningful and fulfilling lives, to cultivate what is best within themselves, and to enhance their experiences of love, work, and play. This, along with a good work life balance, is how Angie manages her daily life.

Alcohol — the Penn State Study

Many people enjoy having a drink after a long day at work to help them relax. It often starts with one drink a day but then for some, alcohol intake gradually increases until before you know it, your after-work drinks become a crutch and you start to get antsy and irritated if you can't have your favorite drink after a long work day.

Penn State researchers in the College of Health and Human Development studied the relationship between stress and drinking. The study was funded by the National Institute on Alcohol and Alcoholism, and results were published in the journal Psychology of Addictive Behaviors.

A total of 744 students at Penn State spent two weeks of every semester, from their first semester through the end of their senior year, filling out daily web-based diary entries about their stress levels and drinking habits. They answered questions about any stress they experienced that day, the cause of said stress, and how many drinks they had that day if any.

"In the fourth year, students were also screened for alcohol problems by using something called AUDIT: the Alcohol Use Disorders Identification Test," said Michael Russell, assistant professor of biobehavioral health. "The students were asked questions about potentially problematic behaviors like not being able to stop drinking once they start or if they often black out while drinking."

The research showed that each additional stressor raised a student's odds of drinking by eight percent, and the amount they drank went up by four percent. On days the students reported drinking without stressors, they had 4.8 drinks on average. On days they reported six stressors, they had 5.9 drinks on average. About 15.7% of all diary entries collected were marked as drinking days, and those days tended to qualify as heavy drinking days.

While this study was conducted using college students, the results are more applicable to working people. As a working person you will be above the legal drinking age and have a steady income to be able to afford alcohol. The stressors of your everyday job are similar to, if not worse than, the stressors of all the work for college classes.

We tend to drink when we want to loosen up or unwind. The purpose of the Penn State study was to show how alcohol is commonly used to relieve stress. The study goes on to show how we can slowly, often without realizing, start to become heavier drinkers, and we can even sometimes turn into alcoholics. Remember to be careful when drinking alcohol, and always keep in mind how much alcohol you're consuming. Be aware of any signs that you may be turning into an alcoholic.

Mental Health

Maintaining good mental health leads to a positive work life balance. Employers often offer paid time off for family emergencies, vacation time, and a few sick days, partly to avoid employees' developing stress and anxiety about personal matters. They also sometimes offer an in-office gym, a quiet space, childcare services, office retreats, and 401(k) plans. Good physical fitness, short breaks throughout the workday, and help taking care of young children are all things that can lead to good positive mental health among workers—and advantages that you should take advantage of when possible.

Even time spent getting to know and bonding with coworkers, and planning for financial security after retirement are contributors to positive mental health. Weekend retreats and after work happy hour events with colleagues are great ways to reinforce connections and build friendships. (Just be conscious of the Penn State study, and remember that it's easier to lose track of how much alcohol you consume if you are drinking at home as opposed to drinking at a bar.)

Two of the easiest ways to take care of your own mental health—to have positive relationships with and understanding of your own emotions and behaviors—are making sure you're not overworking yourself, and talking to someone about what's going on in your mind. Keeping worries, stress, and fears bottled up can lead to an emotional crisis or breakdown.

Quite often, those who don't talk to others about what's troubling them turn to drugs or alcohol as coping mechanisms. Drugs and alcohol create an artificial positive but short-lived feeling in the brain, but that kind of self-medicating often leads to addiction, or possible overdosing which can be fatal—especially if you're alone at home instead of with friends at a bar.

When you notice yourself getting overwhelmed or severely stressed, find someone with whom you can talk about anything. It could be a relative, friend, mentor, or a therapist. They can help you cope by listening to what may be weighing you down, and sharing some of the pain you may be feeling.

You may not know it, but those around you may be suffering from mental health issues. The next time you ask someone how they are doing, really ask them how they are doing. Listen, try to help them with their problems as best as you can, and reassure them that everything is going to be okay and that you are always available and that they can trust you to keep their personal business confidential. However, it is important to remind them that talking to you is no substitute for speaking with a trained and licensed professional.

Keep in mind though that it's okay to focus on yourself first. Don't try to take on other people's problems if you are still learning how to deal with your own. This is one situation in which it's okay to be a bit selfish.

As a society, Americans have usually avoided addressing mental health—except for when a celebrity's mental health makes the news. Many famous people who were once suffering in silence—like Swedish DJ and record producer Avicii (Tim Bergling), comedian and actor Robin Williams, Kurt Cobain—get our attention for a time. In a survey of over 2,000 musicians by Help Musicians UK, over 70% reported suffering from high levels of anxiety and almost 70% reported having experienced depression. The struggles Avicii faced may not be so different from those that Amy Winehouse and Kurt Cobain are known for. Many other celebrities have spoken about the importance of mental health awareness and how mental health issues directly affect them or people they know. However, you don't have to be famous to suffer from mental health issues.

Mental health issues affect people in everyone's lives, friends and relatives who on the surface don't seem to be struggling. Hiding mental health challenges is the norm, unfortunately.

According to Psychology Today, one in four people will face mental health concerns, including college students and young adults—and those who start their own businesses. The

Gallup Wellbeing Index found that 45% of entrepreneurs report being stressed, compared to 42% of people in other professions. Entrepreneurs also report being 34% likely to have worried a lot vs. 30% for other professions According to research published in *the Journal of Small Business Economics* by the UC Berkeley Institutional Review Board, mental health differences directly or indirectly affected 72% of the entrepreneurs in the sample. Also, entrepreneurs were found to be more likely than others to experience depression, ADHD, addiction, and bipolar diagnosis. Colin Kroll, The founder of Vine and HQ Trivia, is one entrepreneur who suffered from mental health problems.

If you find yourself in a situation that you can't handle on your own, don't jeopardize your mental health by staying silent. Seek help.

Signs of Mental Health Issues

Some early warning signs of mental health issues include:

- Eating or sleeping too much or too little. People who sleep too much may be avoiding problems, and people who don't get enough sleep may be overworking which can lead to some issues.

- Pulling away from people and usual activities

- Having low energy or no energy

- Feeling numb or feeling like nothing matters

- Unexplained aches and pains

- Feeling helpless or hopeless

- Smoking, drinking, or using drugs all of a sudden, or more than usual

- Feeling unusually confused, forgetful, on edge, angry, upset, worried, or scared

- Severe mood swings that cause problems in relationships

- Persistent thoughts and memories you can't get out of your head

- Hearing voices or believing things that are not true
- Thinking of harming yourself or others

- Inability to perform one's usual daily tasks like taking care of your kids or getting to work or school

While the above lists early warning signs of mental health issues, remember that it is possible to experience one or more of these symptoms but *not* have mental health issues. It could be a symptom of a different issue, or simply a normal life transition. If you or a family member or close friend is concerned about any symptoms, however, do not to try to self-diagnose yourself, and definitely do not self-medicate. Please talk to a licensed professional instead. Colleges, workplaces, churches, social service agencies, and other entities often provide confidential free or low-cost mental health counseling.

Tim Draper

During the summer of 2016, when I was a rising college sophomore, I had the opportunity to attend Draper University, a Silicon Valley based entrepreneurship bootcamp, started by noted venture capitalist Tim Draper. One of his key pieces of advice for work life balance is "Never get overwhelmed." Now, that is easier said than done, but it is possible. There are steps you can take to ensure you stay calm, cool, and collected most of the time. Draper also recommends, "Take it one step at a time." Don't get bogged down by how many steps a task has or how many things you have to do. Focus on your goals piece by piece.

Draper also advises, "Do the hardest stuff first and everything else seems to go quickly." This is something I try to live by. The final piece of advice which Draper gave me is, "The Hardest time of life is your 20's, and maybe your early 30's, but it gets better because you keep learning more and more." These are our years to explore, learn, and grow, and prepare for the future and everything it has in store.

What's My Plus?

In chapter one, I talked about a job I had, through a third part company, where I was going door to door selling television, phone, and internet for Verizon. While I found it helpful that this particular job had more of a proper schedule than my previous job with Vector Marketing, I found it to take up a lot of time and energy. This was a full-time job during the summer after my sophomore year of college. I found it strenuous to be working for twelve or more hours per day for six days each week, and seven days if we didn't meet our weekly quota in six days. Besides the long hours and lack of days off, the job was also extremely fast paced. We had a very short time in which we had to go from house to house in order to keep up with our daily goal in terms of the number of houses we wanted to hit. I found this to be quite tough for me.

This job wasn't great for work life balance. It was taking up so much of my time and draining my energy. I effectively had little to no personal life due to being too exhausted in what little time I did have to myself. This is when I realized that a job somewhere in between this one and my previous job with Vector Marketing might be ideal for me—a job which wasn't extremely fast paced and time consuming but still had some semblance of a structured schedule to help me keep on task.

Chapter 5 Takeaways

1. Find a work path and a lifestyle that works for you.

2. Manage your time and stress levels in the workplace effectively.

3. Use breaks from work to revitalize and refresh.

4. Take care of your mental health.

5. Know the signs of mental health issues.

6. Don't self-medicate with alcohol or drugs to relieve stress.

7. Don't self-diagnose. Seek professional help.

Chapter 6 - Side Hustles

A side hustle is any job you have in addition to (on the side of) a full-time job. While some side hustles are simply ways to make income, most side hustles relate to a person's passions. If you are earning enough from a full-time job, or fortunate enough to still be supported by parents, a side hustle is a great way to explore bringing a passion to life as a business.

A side hustle is ideal for aspiring entrepreneurs, but is also a wise move for people who can't find a job, and anyone who doesn't want to later regret not having pursued their passions. A side hustle can be as simple as selling your hand-made jewelry online or as complicated as managing a larger business with one or more employees—perhaps something you know you eventually want to turn into a full-time living.

If you don't have a lot of spare money, make your side hustle something with a relatively low startup cost. Remember to look at the level of risk to reward, and that starting a new business is a gamble. Only invest as much as you can afford to lose. While you obviously hope to make a profit on your investment, it's quite possible that it doesn't work out and you lose everything you invested.

Starting a side hustle doing something that's already proven is much less risky than creating a brand new product or service, though you probably won't become an overnight success story. An example of that is turning a knitting hobby into a clothing or accessory brand. Of course, that's been done over and over again, but you can be successful at it if you have a unique twist to offer. That's how successful restaurants pop up every day. They add value to an existing product or service. When taking on a proven business model, it's much easier to show people how and why you can and will be successful with your business.

The brand Supreme has a limited release for all its products, which are often high end unique sneakers. They make sure the amount they release is always less than the demand. While other sneaker companies are notorious for doing this as well, Supreme's niche makes them appealing to a wide audience hungry for their next featured item. I have a friend who routinely buys any new product Supreme puts out so she can then resell them at a profit to Supreme collectors who weren't able to acquire them in the initial release. She sees this as a way for her to make a quick buck while a college student and not something she wants to do for a living. Meanwhile, another friend does this same thing for a variety of fashion brands. While this isn't exactly what he wants to do as a full-time job when he graduates college, this is still very much related to his interests, as he is a fashion major. It's a way for him to make money while keeping up to date with the latest fashion trends. Buying and reselling online is absolutely something that can be done fulltime later on in life.

Another man was looking for a way to make a little extra income while in college. He noticed that all sorts of seasonal items were heavily discounted in the days after a holiday, like Christmas decorations that are marked way down in the days after Christmas. This man started collecting these sorts of seasonal items in his home when they went on sale, then saving them for about a year until they were in season again. What started as a small side hustle eventually outgrew his home because he began buying larger and larger quantities of items on discount until he eventually needed to invest in a storage locker and ultimately decided he could make this little venture his full-time job. This is an example of something that you can do if you need an extra income on the side.

Jamie Siminoff

Some businesses start by accident. Take the Ring video doorbell, created by Jamie Siminoff, for example. Siminoff was always an inventor at heart. He would spend long amounts of time in his garage tinkering on various invention ideas. When Siminoff's wife, Erin, complained that Siminoff couldn't hear the doorbell ring from the garage, he invented the Ring video doorbell–a doorbell with a built in camera that streams to the owner's phone.

At that time, Siminoff didn't think much of the product beyond a means to be able to hear and answer the doorbell from his garage while tinkering on other ideas. In fact, he believed that people would simply write off his creation as $200 toy. However, Erin convinced him that the Ring video doorbell was in fact going to be his hit product, and she was right. Siminoff drained his bank account to cover the first order of five thousand Ring video doorbells. It was not without a lot of hard work to improve the quality of Siminoff's product, but his company was eventually bought by Amazon for an estimated value of between $1.2 billion and $1.8 billion dollars. Siminoff even did a lot of work himself to get large investors and to get his product in stores before his company was able to be acquired.

When the product initially launched, people dismissed it as more of a toy or geeky gadget as opposed to a practical security measure. Just as Siminoff had feared himself. Also, when Siminoff brought this product to Shark Tank in search of an investment, Kevin O'Leary was the only shark to make him an offer which Siminoff ended up turning down. However, Siminoff went on to convince investors like Richard Branson and Hamet Watt of Upfront Ventures that Ring is a good home security tool since you can see who is ringing your doorbell even when you are not home. In what seemed almost like the blink of an eye, but was actually a number of years of hard work, Siminoff's Ring video doorbell had gone from a side hustle to a full-time business to being sold to Amazon.

Create for one to reach millions

Authenticity

If you are a fledgling inventor or product developer, strive to create for yourself first and not for others. It's easy to forget why you started creating in the first place if you become too focused on pleasing others—and it's impossible to please everyone. You may start to become displeased with your efforts if you focus on creating for others, as it will no longer be your authentic work. Authenticity means creating something you can be proud of regardless of what anyone else thinks of it. You still know for yourself that you put in your best effort, and you like the final result even if everyone else hates it.

Be Yourself

Don't try to emulate your favorite person or any particular leader in your field. Everyone is different. You need to be the best version of yourself. You won't be the next Steve

Jobs or the next Picasso, but you can be the best version of yourself because nobody knows you like you know yourself. That being said, it is not only okay, but it is suggested to look at the habits of your favorite successful people and adopt some of their habits. For example, you may like that Arianna Huffington always sets an intention for her day, but you may prefer to set it the night before rather than the morning of. In cases like this, you are adopting some habits that have worked for business leaders but changing them to work for you. You are not just completely copying anyone's habits, because they will not work for you the exact way they work for anyone else.

Steve Jobs gave the 2005 Stanford University commencement address in which he had to say, "Your work is going to fill a large part of your life, and the only way to be truly satisfied is to do what you believe is great work. And the only way to do great work is to love what you do. If you haven't found it yet, keep looking. Don't settle. As with all matters of the heart, you'll know when you find it."

Jobs is essentially saying that you will be happiest if you can make a career out of what you love. Don't settle. If you love sports but aren't athletic, consider sports management or becoming a sports commentator. If you love trying new foods but aren't a chef, try starting a blog about food, or becoming a food critic. With patience and some radical thinking, there's a way to make almost any dream a reality.

Making a lot of money is great, but doing what you love is even better. But why settle? You can potentially make a lot of money if you truly love what you do and if you're good at it. The last thing you want is to feel like you lived an unfulfilling life when you're older because you didn't truly love the job you had. According to the World Health Organization, people spend, on average, one third of their life working. That's a lot of time. Why not spend that time doing something fulfilling that you can say you enjoyed beyond your paycheck?

In the commencement address, Jobs also said, "Your time is limited, so don't waste it living someone else's life. Don't be trapped by dogma—which is living with the results of other people's thinking. Don't let the noise of others' opinions drown out your own inner voice. And most important, have the courage to follow your heart and intuition."

Jobs is saying that you should strive to be the best version of yourself. Be who you want to be. Not what anyone else says you should be. Doing this will allow you to become other people's favorite person. Don't let anyone try to dictate to you how you should live your life. You're the only person who is going to be spending 24 hours per day with you. Also, attempting to emulate your favorite person will only make you look like a copy of them. Don't try to be like your college professor who you admire or like that classmate of yours who seems to be doing so well at everything. You should be the best version of you that you can be.

Document. Don't Create
Fans and followers will come and go, but at the end of the day, the only person who you can count on to always be there is yourself. That's why it's important to put in what feels like your best effort. Entrepreneur, author, speaker, and internet personality Gary Vaynerchuck says, "I'll give you the biggest tip when it comes to content creation: **Document. Don't create.**"

The phrase "Document. Don't create" is a simple phrase. What Vaynerchuck means is to document your journey rather than being caught up in worries about what content to create to connect with your audience. Imagine, for example, that you want to be a professional dancer. Don't worry about how good of a dancer you are or what kind of dance styles people like. Document your journey of practicing dance, or whatever it is you have to offer people. People appreciate you being authentic and real with them. Nobody is perfect, and your audience knows this, so you certainly don't need to try to make it seem like you're perfect.

Vaynerchuck encourages his followers to separate the work you've done from the final results. Your video, book, or song may only get a few hits, but you have to still be able to say that you genuinely put in your best work. Sometimes you may be one part of a larger project in which someone else screws up their part. As a result, the final project may not turn out well, but you need to remain confident in the fact that you truly put forth *your* best effort.

Don't let your audience control you

Imagine you are creating a weekly video series but not getting many views. Keep putting forth your best work and the audience will eventually come. Nobody is perfect, so you can always learn new things to improve your skills or expand them. It is okay to take suggestions from your audience, but remember to always create something you genuinely believe in. It is usually quite obvious to your audience when you genuinely like what you're doing and when you don't. You will start to lose interest in your project if you focus too hard on pleasing your audience, turning your efforts into less and less of what you wanted, in an attempt to make it what the fans want. Remember, it's impossible to please everyone.

You can only be the best version of yourself. That is what will make you better each day in order to eventually connect you with your audience. Comparing yourself to anyone else or trying to create what others want will only stop you from progressing.

Stop Comparing Yourself to Others

Life isn't always fair. You probably know someone who was born into better circumstances than you. At the same time, someone probably looks at you and envies the circumstances you were born into. Someone born into a middle-class family, living in a decent neighborhood with good schools, and parents who make enough might be the envy of someone born into a poor family just getting by on minimum-wage jobs, wishing they were living comfortably like the middle-class family. Meanwhile, the middle-class family might be jealous of a rich family who has more money than they know what to do with. Yet none of those financial statuses have anything to do with which person is the happiest. Money can buy you a lot of useful things, but it can't buy it true happiness. It can only buy you temporary artificial happiness.

What's My Plus?

I've been very lucky. My parents paid my tuition and supported me all through college, though like any student, I could always use some extra spending money. That's why I took the jobs I've mentioned (selling knives and cable TV services).

I also thought about other ways to make money, like buying candy, chips, and soda in bulk, then selling them cheaper than usually available on campus. I knew that would work and require minimal effort, but since I didn't, strictly speaking, need the cash, I realized I was free to pursue my hobbies and passions and then later on, if my passion project succeeded, I could think about how to possibly monetize it.

When I founded Visionaries Film Festival, my intention was not to personally profit, but to have an experience doing something I was extremely interested in, gain new skills, and explore what might be possible to achieve on my own. Every cent collected for the film festival to date has been reinvested towards improving and expanding the event for the next year. My goal is to showcase the highest quality of film possible, but more than that I want it to be a platform to help showcase student filmmakers and other new young filmmakers. With this project, I've seen the wisdom in the adage that when your long-term goals align with your short-term projects, you can make a bigger impact over a long period of time.

I started Visionaries Film Festival in 2019. I ran the first Visionaries Film Festival mostly on my own with occasional help from one more person. While in college, I worked at several local film festivals and even had an opportunity to visit South by South West in Austin, Texas during my senior year spring break. While working at film festivals over the years, I not only got an inside glimpse into how film festivals operate, but I also met many seasoned industry professionals. Some of whom would later mentor me when I started Visionaries Film Festival.

Starting Visionaries Film Festival was lower risk for me than it might be for others. While I had every intention to raise the money on my own to run the film festival, I knew that I had my parents financial support if I feel short of operating costs. Luckily, I found a reasonably priced venue, and was able to recoup slightly more than my operating costs through sponsorships, ad sales, and ticket sales.

I ran the first Visionaries Film Festival mostly on my own but with occasional help from one other person. Initially, I didn't want to take on this project alone. However, I also didn't want to give myself any reasons not to start my own film festival, so I went ahead and started it on my own. I was terrified, but at the same time, I was confident in my abilities to quickly learn, to adapt when necessary, and to put on a quality film festival. In 2019, Visionaries Film Festival was a one day event. In 2020, I had to learn how to do the Film Festival online due to the global spread of COVID-19. Taking Visionaries Film Festival virtual wasn't such a bad thing. With lower operating costs I was able to put on a three day event.

I fully realize that I had many advantages other college students and new graduates don't. Had I needed to earn money throughout college, I'm sure I would have had different experiences. Yet I believe that when it comes to setting yourself apart, creating your Plus, starting side hustles, and becoming an entrepreneur, where you begin is less important than what you do next.

If, like Jobs advised, you want your passion to turn into your life's work, making that happen has far less to do with your family of origin and far more dependent on what you make of opportunities along the way, and your commitment to developing your own work path.

Chapter 6 Takeaways

1. A side hustle is ideal for aspiring entrepreneurs, people who are out of work, and those who want to pursue their passions.

2. Listen to advice: you may already have created a winning product or idea.

3. Find mentors, study others who have succeeded, keep perfecting your skills and craft.

4. But, please yourself first. Create for yourself. Not for others.

5. Be your authentic self in all your endeavors.

6. Nobody knows you like you know yourself.

Chapter 7 - From Side Hustle to Full-time

You may have known for a while that you want to turn your side hustle into a full-time job, but are unsure of the right time to do this. There are a few key indicators that help you know when exactly that right time is. My friend Summer Silvery, a full time freelance graphic artist, figured out how to do this for herself. You'll see her story later on in this chapter.

You need to look at your time and how you're spending it. When you start a side hustle based on a passion, you'll likely spend all your spare time working on it—nights, weekends, maybe even mornings before work or school. At some point, you may notice that you are unable to grow your side hustle any further without investing your full time attention into it. This is a critical moment; you have to decide if it's better for you to quit your full-time job or hire someone to help you continue to grow your side hustle. (Just remember that nobody who works for you will ever be as passionate about your business as you are. If they are, you're probably in the wrong business.)

Money

Though your side hustle may be generating income, you may not be making enough money from it to be able to able to quit your full-time job. While you might have enough savings to last you until such a time when your side hustle is bringing in as much money as, or more than, your full-time job, you still need to reassess your finances. See how you can lower your expenses. Spend less money going out, buy less expensive clothes (last season's styles on discount or non-name brand), and even consider downsizing your home or selling some of your possessions if you can. Try out living more frugally for a few months, to see if you can do it; this will simulate what life will be like once that full-time paycheck is gone.

It may be easier to turn your side hustle into a full-time career if it is related to your current full-time job or a previous job you have held. That way, you may already have a list of potential clients that you can bring with you, a network to tap. Plus, you will have built up credibility in that profession and already have all the skills necessary to succeed.

Alternative Jobs

If you really want to quit your full-time job to focus more on your side hustle, but you don't have enough money saved, consider switching to a full-time job that allows for more flexibility in your schedule. There might even be a way to alter your current full-time job, if your company is open to flexible working hours or working remotely from home. Or, you might ask about scaling back from being a full-time to a part time employee.

Freelance jobs allow for maximum flexibility. Part-time jobs are less flexible but obviously still give you more free time than a full-time job. Short-term, one-off, and temporary or seasonal jobs are also good ways to have more time to focus on your side hustle without having to completely give up a paying job. Some examples of seasonal jobs include summer camps, summer lifeguard, Christmas or Halloween shops, or any businesses that increases staff around certain seasons or holidays. Some examples of freelance jobs include dog walking, tutoring, babysitting, musical lessons, food delivery, and driving for companies like Uber and Lyft. These types of jobs allow you to take create your own hours, and take on more or less work depending on how much time your side hustle business demands.

Loss of Benefits

Before quitting a full-time job to turn your side hustle into a full-time work, consider what else you might be giving up besides the paycheck. When you start your own business, you will no longer have health insurance sponsored by your employer, nor will you have paid time off for vacation or sick days. If you or your significant other has a baby, there will also be no paid maternity leave. Your employer may also be paying into a retirement fund, or providing other tangible benefits like sponsored child care, gym membership, or life insurance. Remember to factor these things into your expenses (or decide that you're willing to forgo some or all of them) before quitting your full-time job.

Expenses

If you're going to start a new business or expand a smaller one, you must know the associated laws and regulations. Make sure everything you are planning to do is 100% legal. Know the applicable restrictions. Laws vary by country and by state: certain things may be legal in one area of the country but may not be legal elsewhere.

Imagine you want to start a marijuana dispensary. In Colorado, you can operate a recreational marijuana dispensary; you can even apply for a marijuana license online in Colorado. However, in New York and New Jersey marijuana sales are only legal for medical use, not recreational. States like these also have a very limited number of licenses available for marijuana businesses as well as a lot of red tape to navigate to obtain one of these licenses.

Every business will have initial administrative, marketing, insurance, and perhaps supply or inventory costs. These include a website, purchasing initial equipment, professional services (like an accountant), transportation or shipping, and rent if you need an outside workspace. If you need to hire an attorney to handle any legal matters or contracts associated with start-up, factor in that expense.

If you are going to be hiring employees for your business, know the costs associated, including health insurance; employer contributions to Social Security, disability and unemployment; liability insurance. Learn how much these are going to cost before hiring and determine if you can afford to do so. If your need for help doesn't require full-time employees, consider instead hiring freelancers or independent contractors (but know the law; you can't hire a full-time employee and call them a freelancer just to avoid federal requirements).

Before quitting their full-time jobs, most people set goals for where they want to take their side hustle. For a side business that is generating a steady amount of money month after month, your goal might be reaching a certain higher minimum income per month before quitting your full-time job. This amount may be the same amount you are making from your full-time job, or it may even be higher to cover associated costs and loss of benefits. For side businesses where the monthly income keeps changing, you may set a goal for yourself of consistently increasing income month after month, so that eventually it exceeds what you are making from your full-time job. That may be your target to make yourself feel comfortable enough to quit your full-time job.

Summer Silvery

When I was a full-time student, I always put my education before everything else. College was essentially my full-time job. Finding a job to fit into my crazy class schedule was often tough, and sometimes felt next to impossible. Yet, I was still able to find a way to work jobs and internships into my schedule.

Many students have unique journeys, and some of them document it along the way, sharing their experiences and simultaneously inspiring others to do the same. What's even more incredible is that some of these people have figured out ways to monetize their personal journey and create an income from simply living their lives and sharing it with others who may share similar interests.

Summer Silvery, a friend of mine, quit college and moved to Silicon Valley briefly before moving to Los Angeles to pursue both her lifelong dream of living in Los Angeles and her passion for drawing. Summer moved to Silicon Valley where she was a student at the Draper University entrepreneurship boot camp program. That's where Summer and I met. She decided to document her journey and launched Tenacious Ones. She's documented her journey of moving from Ohio to Silicon Valley to LA and becoming a full-time digital artist.

Summer and I went through Draper University's Summer 2016 program along with roughly 50 other entrepreneurs from all over the world, all of us living together and spending a lot of time forming what might be lifelong friendships and partnerships.

Of her time there, Summer notes, "Because of Draper University, I learned how much I am capable of. I learned how there is NOTHING to learn when you're always limiting yourself to the same day to day routine. Stepping outside of your comfort zone and experiencing new things ALL of the time, knowing that failing at things is OKAY, because without it, how would we learn? This stuff is what sets us up to have a life with no regrets. This is what makes you smile every morning and throughout your day because you whole-heartedly know you're doing everything you can for what you want most out of life. I will forever be grateful for Draper University because it brought out everything I already had within me, at such a larger capacity than I could have ever imagined for myself."

Summer started making videos documenting her journey. She also documents all the challenges and struggles she faces throughout her journey. Summer realized that all her struggles were something commonly felt by others, and she wanted to pull back the veil to be raw and transparent. She knew that what she learned from her struggles could help others.

With Tenacious Ones, Summer started making videos for YouTube to talk about her struggles and how she overcame them. She knew others would be able to relate. She also writes about the same things on the blog she maintains on her Tenacious Ones website.

Because she is being completely real with people and talking about relatable things, Summer is starting to gain a following which she could monetize if she wanted to. As summer's social media following grows, she can introduce paid posts and general ads to supplement her income aside from her always growing digital art business. Though, she prefers to keep it 100% authentic without any ads for now. Aside from being completely transparent and sharing her struggles with her social media followers, Summer also helps brands create logos and promotional materials. This is how Summer monetizes her passion for drawing. She's even created her own series of children's books.

Summer's story isn't all that unheard of. You've heard of people like Steve Jobs and Mark Zuckerberg who dropped out of college to pursue their passions. However, there are so many kids who dropped out of college who you have never heard about. The ones who's plans didn't work out. If you truly feel like college is a waste of your time and money, make sure that you have a solid game plan before dropping out. If everything fails, you won't have a college degree to fall back on and it may prove to be very tough to find a full time job. And if you decide to go back to college to finish your degree, you will have lost that time in between.

Overall, for any business, you need to be authentic and passionate. Occasionally you will experience waves when your product or service is higher in popularity. You may be featured on a front page or written about in a prominent blog. While you will get new followers, many likes on a post, and maybe even some additional sales, don't let all of that get to your head. Remember that it's a wave, and soon will ebb. However, the fans will stick around if you put out work you are passionate about. If you can do it, there's an audience for it, so get out there and keep living your passions. You only have one life, so make the most of it.

What's My Plus?

My side hustle running a film festival hasn't turned full-time nor do I expect that it will, but that's not to say it couldn't. I started Visionaries Film Festival as a hobby. After several years of volunteering with and working at film festivals, I had an idea of a different kind of festival I could start on my own. My intention was to create a platform to showcase student filmmakers and other first-time filmmakers. I wanted them to know that if they can create a film, there is an audience out there interested in watching it. I didn't start the festival with the intention of it becoming a full-time job post college. However, I fully know that I could grow it into a full-time career in the future if I invest my time and effort to that end. Or, perhaps I could hire someone else to run it. For now though, it simply continues to grow year after year. The number of films submitted keeps increasing as well as the quality of the films, and the attendance at Visionaries Film Festival film screenings keeps increasing as well. Being a seasonal event, the film festival doesn't take up a lot of my time. Thankfully, the bulk of the work is in the few weeks leading up to and the few weeks after the event. I am able to dedicate time in the evenings after work and on weekends to Visionaries Film Festival. As of now, I am sticking with it, and that is really all I can do.

Chapter 7 Takeaways

1. Unique ventures may be overnight sensations, but more common ventures can tap into a larger, already-established market.

2. Alternative jobs can free up time to transition your side hustle into a full-time job while ensuring a source of income.

3. Before quitting your job, weigh the loss of employer-sponsored benefits in addition to loss of salary.

4. Consider startup costs and legal matters related to turning a side hustle into a serious full-time job.

5. Tap into your existing network. Friends and family already around you may be more helpful and useful to you than you realize.

Letter From The Author

Congratulations! You've made it this far, exploring how to create your own Plus, and the possibilities that exist for you as a college student or full-time worker pursuing a side hustle. Thank you for taking the time to read this book. I hope you have found the lessons and stories I shared to be of value. If you found any part of this book helpful, I would truly appreciate it if you shared it with anyone else you think could benefit.

Rather than feeling overwhelmed by all the tips and perhaps new ideas you encountered in these pages, think about only what you can take away and are ready to try in your own life. Only do what you feel comfortable doing. Start small and gradually work your way up to more daunting tasks. If you try something and it doesn't fell right or work for you, you can pivot. While the tips mentioned in this book work for most people, they won't necessarily work for everyone. Creating your own plus is not a one size fits all approach. That's why there are so many options.

My intention with this book is for it to be something you can return to at several stages, depending on where you are in the college or work journey. While this book details how to balance a job or side hustle with college, and how to turn that side hustle into a business, perhaps you don't currently need or want that experience. Your circumstances and dreams will shift though, as you move ahead, so you might return to these ideas when you are ready to try something different. Whatever you decide is best for you is exactly what you should do.

I would love to hear your thoughts. Tell me how this book has personally helped you. You can email me at WhatsYourPlusBook@gmail.com, direct message me on Instagram @TheVihanKhanna, or connect with me on LinkedIn at LinkedIn.com/in/VihanKhanna. Also, please consider leaving a review on Amazon any other website.

Thanks again for spending some time with me here. I will know I've made a difference if I am able to help even just one person a little bit. Here's hoping you have a happy journey!

Vihan Khanna

Sources

"120 Years of American Education: A Statistical Portrait." *National Center for Education Statistics*, US Department of Education Office of Educational Research and Improvement, Jan. 1993.

Adams, Susan. "The Exclusive Inside Story Of Ring: From 'Shark Tank' Reject To Amazon's Latest Acquisition." *Forbes*, Forbes, 27 Feb. 2018.

Ali, Shainna. "What No One Wants To Say About Avicii's Passing." *Psychology Today*, Psychology Today.

"Bachelor's Degree Holders among Individuals 25–44 Years Old | State Indicators | NSF - National Science Foundation." *National Center for Science and Engineering Statistics*, National Science Foundation, 29 Apr. 2020.

Bohn, Katie. "Drinking to Cope with Stress May Increase Risk of Alcohol Problems." *Penn State News*, Penn State University.

Bustamante, Jaleesa. "College Graduation Statistics [2020]: Total Graduates per Year." *EducationData*, EducationData, 2019.

Clifford, Cat. "Elon Musk's Morning Routine and Top Productivity Tip." *CNBC*, CNBC, 21 June 2017.

Goodman, Nadia. "How to Train Your Brain to Multitask Effectively." *Entrepreneur*, Entrepreneur, 25 Feb. 2013.

Kruse, Kevin. "The Jack Dorsey Productivity Secret That Enables Him To Run Two Companies At Once." *Forbes*, Forbes, 12 Oct. 2015.

Orendorff, Aaron. "The Dark Side of Entrepreneurship with Data & Resources for Help." *Shopify Plus*, Shopify.

Suazo, Amanda. "How to Meal Prep For Beginners: Everything You Need to Know." *Bulletproof*, Bulletproof, 20 Sept. 2020.

The Oracles. "10 Morning Routines of Wildly Successful Entrepreneurs." *SUCCESS*, SUCCESS, 9 Feb. 2017.

Townsend, Brad. "How Mark Cuban Went from Beer-Stained Floors, Flat Broke to Billions." *The Dallas Morning News*, The Dallas Morning News, 16 Apr. 2011.

Turczynski, Bart. "2020 HR Statistics: Job Search, Hiring, Recruiting & Interviews." *Zety*, Zety, 15 Nov. 2016.

Vaynerchuck, Gary. "Document, Don't Create: Creating Content That Builds Your Personal Brand." *GaryVaynerchuk.Com*, Gary Vaynerchuck.

Walton, Alice G. "The Morning Habits Of Highly Successful People." *Forbes*, Forbes, 29 Jan. 2016.

"What Is Mental Health?" *MentalHealth.Gov*.

Made in the USA
Monee, IL
18 December 2020

54319396R00059